A page from J. B. Waring's 'Masterpieces at the International Exhibition, 1862', showing some of the Minton ornamental ware exhibited there.

MINTON

Joan Jones

Shire Publications Ltd

CONTENTS

Copyright © 1995 by Royal Doulton Limited.
First published 1992; second edition 1995.
Shire Album 279. ISBN 0 7478 0304 8.

Printed in Great Britain by C. I. T Printing
Services, Press Buildings, Merlins Bridge,
Haverfordwest, Dyfed SA61 1XF.

British Library Cataloguing in Publication Data: Jones, Joan. Minton. — (Shire Albums Series;
No. 279). I. Title. II. Series. 738.09. ISBN 0-7478-0304-8.

ACKNOWLEDGEMENTS
The author wishes to pay tribute to the many people who, past and present, have loved and
preserved the traditions of Minton. In writing this book she has been helped and supported by
many people but there is space to mention only a few. She is particularly grateful to her
colleagues in the Royal Doulton Company, especially members of the Corporate Communica-
tions Department — Ann Linscott, Mary Moorcroft and Valerie Baynton for advice and encour-
agement, and Anita Fitchett for her expertise in setting out the manuscript. Special thanks are
due to Ann Hughes for her help and enthusiasm; to Alyn Giles Jones, who catalogued the Minton
Archives; and to the author's husband, Lionel Jones, who has been a constant support. The
author also expresses her thanks to Gerald Wells of Northern Counties Photographers for his
usual patience and attention. She is grateful to Royal Doulton Limited for supplying many of the
photographs, and to the individuals and organisations listed below for their kind permission to
reproduce photographs.
  Illustrations are acknowledged as follows: Britannia, Grays Antique Market, page 26 (all) and
27 (left); Christies, pages 21 (left) and 23 (top); G. Godden, pages 7 (bottom), 9 and 20 (top
right); Thomas Goode and Company Limited, page 21 (right); H. V. Levy, page 6 (top left);
Metropolitan Museum of Art (Robert L. Isaacson Gift), page 20 (top left); Minton Museum,
Royal Doulton Limited, cover and pages 1-5 (all), 6 (top right and bottom left), 8 (bottom), 10, 11
(bottom), 12-13 (all), 15 (all), 16 (top two), 17, 18 (top left), 19, 20 (bottom), 22 (both), 23
(middle), 24 (top right and centre), 25, 27 (top right and bottom) and 28-32 (all); Phillips, pages 7
(top), 8 (top) and 18 (bottom); Sotheby's, pages 18 (top right), 23 (bottom) and 24 (top left). The
illustrations on pages 11 (top), 14 (both) and 16 (bottom) are from private collections.

*Left: The Council Bronze
Medal was awarded to Minton
at the Great Exhibition of 1851
for 'beauty and originality of
design'.*

*Cover: This cream tureen, a
combination of Parian and
bone china, forms part of the
116-piece dessert service purchased for 1000 guineas by
Queen Victoria at the Great
Exhibition, 1851. 27 cm (11¾
inches).*

First-period bone-china teawares. (Left) Tea bowl and saucer, pattern 791, c.1810. (Top) 'Canoe' or 'New Oval' teapot, pattern 158, c.1805. (Right) Teapot, pattern 678, c.1810.

THOMAS MINTON — THE FOUNDER

Thomas Minton was born at Wyle Cop, Shrewsbury, Shropshire, in 1765. He became an apprentice copperplate engraver under the supervision of Thomas Turner at the Caughley Porcelain Works, Broseley, Shropshire, and soon after completing his apprenticeship he established himself as an engraver in London. Around 1789 he moved to Stoke in Staffordshire to be nearer to his best customers, Josiah Spode, Josiah Wedgwood and the Adams Brothers, and to gain commissions from other pottery manufacturers.

The demand for Thomas Minton's engravings prompted him to consider producing pottery in his own right. In 1793 he purchased a plot of land in London Road, Stoke, and erected a biscuit oven and some working sheds. In the early days Thomas was assisted by Joseph and Samuel Poulson, who produced pottery at the Stone Works nearby. In 1796 Thomas took Joseph Poulson into partnership and the business became known as 'Minton and Poulson'. Soon afterwards, when William Pownall, a Liverpool merchant, invested

capital in the business, the name changed to 'Minton, Poulson and Pownall'.

Between 1798 and 1799 Thomas purchased 84 acres (34 ha) of land on Hendra Common in Cornwall where there was an abundance of china clay and stone which ensured a constant supply of raw materials. Early Minton production concentrated on underglaze blue-printed earthenwares such as the 'Broseley' and 'Willow' patterns of the type he engraved whilst he was at Caughley.

UNDERGLAZE BLUE-PRINTED EARTHENWARES

The copperplates listed in the 1810 and 1817 inventories provide an insight into the type of patterns produced at the time. Dinner and dessert wares included 'Lily', 'Roman', 'Windsor Castle', 'Brick' and 'Rose and Flower'; teawares included 'Cottage', 'Turkish Figure', 'India' and 'Nelson'; toiletwares 'Grotto' and 'Maypole'; and toy wares 'Chinese Figures' and 'Pagoda'. Minton wares were sold to other manufacturers, and through Thomas

3

Dish and cover, underglaze blue-printed and gilded earthenware, 'Dacca' pattern, 'M & B' mark (1836-41).

Minton's brother Arthur, who had a London shop, and other retailers throughout Great Britain and North America.

Early earthenwares were unmarked, making identification difficult. However, around 1830, the monograms of the various partnerships — 'M', 'M & Co', 'M & B' and 'M & H' — can be seen amid a foliate cartouche containing the pattern number or name.

BONE CHINA

About 1798 cream-coloured earthenware and bone china were introduced. Thomas Minton was very proud of his bone-china body. In good humour, he told Dick Hammersley, the dipper: 'This is my body, and not any body! How do you make that out, Dick?' Production of Minton bone china is thought to have ceased in 1816. This was probably due to the slump in exports in the years following the Napoleonic Wars. However, by 1822, when the national economy began to improve, Minton resumed bone-china production.

Tea bowls, breakfast cups, tea cups (with handles, without handles, with high handles) and coffee cans in plain, fluted, 'shankered' or shankered fluted shapes were produced. Caudle cups with stands in 'new' shape were supplied with or without covers. Teapots were produced in three

(Left) 'Bute' shape teacup and saucer, pattern 51, with painted retailer's name of Donovan, c.1800. (Centre) 'Bute' shape teacup and saucer, pattern 299, c.1805. (Right) 'Shankered flute' coffee can, pattern 20, c.1800.

sizes in round, oval plain, oval fluted and square shapes. Coffee pots were made in two sizes. Designs were varied: French-inspired florals, neo-classical, chinoiserie, Imari (rich Japanese style), geometric, harlequin, figure and landscape. Some patterns were highly original — cut orange and lemon slices, orange and gilt flames, and *trompe l'oeil*! Bone-china teawares were painted with a pattern number on the reverse, and from 1810 to 1816 a Sèvres-type mark (two cursive Ls) above an M was added.

In 1808 Joseph Poulson died and John Turner, a potter, of William and John Turner of Lane End, succeeded him. John Turner took responsibility for improvements in the Minton body and glazes. In 1817 Thomas Minton took his two sons into partnership, and the company title changed to 'Thomas Minton and Sons'. Thomas Webb Minton, the elder son, was allocated the clerical work, and Herbert, who was the Minton representative, did 'everything else', according to a contem-

Pattern 126 from the first-period Minton pattern book, olive ground with cut orange slices and purple and yellow leaves, c.1800.

porary of his. The partnership was dissolved on 1st January 1823, and the title reverted to 'Thomas Minton'. This was probably because Thomas Webb Minton entered the church. Herbert remained at the factory but was no longer a partner in the business.

(Left) Caudle cup and stand, shape number 55, c.1830. (Centre) Chocolate cup with cover and stand, pattern 539, c.1810. (Right) Pattern 180, c.1805.

Left: *Bisque figure of 'La Belle Louise', number 154, modelled by G. Cocker, 1835; 21.4 cm (8¹/₂ inches). This figure was also produced in white Parian and in coloured and gilt Parian.*

Right: *Early bone-china figures, c.1830. (Left) 'Spanish Guitar Player', 18.5 cm (7¹/₄ inches). (Top) 'Chamois Hunter', chimney figure number 6, 13 cm (5¹/₄ inches). (Right) 'Don Quixote', chimney figure number 8, 13 cm (5¹/₄ inches). (Bottom) 'Good Night', figure number 12, 9 cm (3¹/₂ inches).*

FIGURES

A series of numbered figures was introduced about 1826. Subjects included royal, political, religious, theatrical, historical, mythological and contemporary characters. George Cocker, John Whittaker and

Pen and ink drawings from the Minton figure books, c.1852, depicting Lord Ronald Gower and Lord Albert Gower.

Edward and Samuel Keys were among the modellers who came to Minton from Derby; this explains the similarity between Minton and Derby figures such as 'Good Night', 'Infant Samuel', 'Hannah More' and 'Wilberforce'. Some early figures were modelled with recessed backs to enable them to sit against a chimney breast, including 'Mother Goose', 'Chamois Hunter', 'Sancho Panza' and 'Don Quixote'. Probably the most amusing were the 'nodding' figures of 'Easy Johnny' and 'Coachee', which were so called because their heads were separate and fixed to bronze weights, which enabled them to nod or shake from side to side. Other figures were made in *bisque* (unglazed bone china) or were decorated in on-glaze enamel and gilt. Some bisque models, including 'Fanny Ellsler', 'Taglioni', 'Ophelia' and 'Cleopatra', were adorned with ruffles and lace. Although many early examples were

6

unmarked, attribution is possible through the figure books, which are illustrated with pen and ink drawings of each figure, with titles and numbers.

ORNAMENTAL WARES

A numbered sequence of ornamental wares was introduced about 1826, to compete with those produced in Europe and to supply the demands of the newly emerging middle class. Identification of early ornamental wares is difficult: copies of Meissen, Sèvres and Chelsea were produced, some having a Meissen blue crossed-swords mark; but Minton wares can usually be confirmed by reference to the Minton ornamental-shape books, which illustrate in pen and ink or sepia photograph form each ornamental piece with its title, number and measurements. Ornaments include 'French Bouquet Pot', 'French Bottle', 'Dresden Match Pot', 'Dresden Candlestick', 'Sèvres Festoon Vase' and 'Gothic Pedestal Ornament'.

From 1823 to the time of Thomas Minton's death in 1836 sales of Minton ware almost doubled, reaching £48,446 *per annum*. The factory wage book dated between 1831 and 1836 recorded slip makers, throwers, turners, handlers, dish and plate makers, scollopers, stencillers, pressers, drab pressers and figurers, modellers and flowerers, hilt and cockspur makers, mould makers, saggar makers, biscuit-ware people, painters, paintresses, gilders, burnishers, engravers, printers with apprentices and assistants, overlookers, kiln people, glost-oven people, clerks, warehouse people, bricklayers, carters and odd men. The precise number of employees cannot be given because many worked in teams and the number in each team was not always recorded.

Bone-china hand-painted 'Gothic Pedestal Ornaments', c.1840.

7

Above: *Bone-china hand-painted ornamental wares in the revived rococo style, c.1840.*

Left: *Stoneware relief-moulded Bacchanalian jug, c.1850.*

Bone-china 'New Tray', shape 245, after the Sèvres plateau Hébert entitled 'Virgin with Child', painted by John Simpson, c.1840; 32 cm (12³/₄ inches) diameter.

HERBERT MINTON — THE INNOVATIVE LEADER

Herbert Minton had no financial interest in the business. Nevertheless, as his father grew older he came to rely upon Herbert, who devoted all his energies to running the company. The reading of his father's will came as a dreadful shock to Herbert. His elder brother, Thomas Webb Minton (who had left the factory twelve years previously), was named as chief beneficiary of his father's estate and as the owner of Minton China and Earthenware Works. Herbert Minton was heard to say: 'If it had not been for my mother and my sisters, I would have given up the potting business.'

Realising the unfairness of the document, Thomas Webb surrendered £23,000, enabling the executors to fund a new partnership between Herbert Minton and John Boyle. John Boyle, who originated from a local potting family, provided business contacts in America and Europe. Trading began as 'Minton and Boyle' in November 1836 but in 1841 the partnership was dissolved, probably because of Boyle's political inclinations and other differences. In 1845 a new partnership was formed with Michael Daintry Hollins, Herbert Minton's nephew by marriage and the grandson of Samuel Hollins, the potter of the New Hall Porcelain Company.

At this period, the shapes and decoration of Minton ornamental wares were influenced by the revived rococo style. Curvaceous shapes were painted with landscapes, fruit and flowers against rich ground colours and were further embellished with a profusion of relief flower encrustations. However, production centred on tableware in bone china, earthenware and ironstone, and on relief-moulded stoneware. From 1842 year ciphers were stamped into the body, and relief-moulded cartouches containing a number and a cursive M were introduced on stonewares and Parian tablewares.

Herbert Minton refused to mark the Minton name on his factory's wares before 1846 but was finally persuaded to do so by Sir Henry Cole, leader of the Design Reform Movement. Cole asked Minton to make a tea-set which he had designed. It was entered in the 1846 Royal Society of Arts competition under the pseudonym of 'Felix Summerly'. One of the conditions of entry specified that manufacturers' names should be clearly marked on all items submitted. Herbert feared that he might upset the china retailers, who preferred their wares to be unmarked, but reluctantly agreed to mark the tea-set with his name.

The tea-set won a silver medal and greatly interested the Prince Consort, who particularly approved of the novelty of the milk jug, which had three lips, enabling the liquid to be poured right or left by a slight movement of the wrist, thus eliminating the necessity to lift the arm. Cole had designed the set for ease of manufacture — spending three days at Minton studying the processes — and for ease of use. The decoration was drawn from historical sources. The successful union between designer and manufacturer proved by the sale of thousands of 'Felix Summerly' tea-sets played a significant role in the development of plans for the Great Exhibition of 1851. Herbert Minton was a major exhibitor and one of the original guarantors of the Great Exhibition, depositing £10,000. (A letter in the Minton Archives signed by Prince Albert bears witness to this.)

Impressed year ciphers used between 1842 and 1942. (From c.1920 to 1968 the number of the month and the last two digits of the year were impressed.)

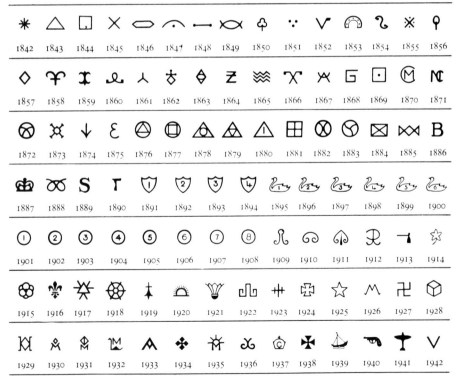

Above: *Parian figure of 'Prince Alfred with Pony', figure number 357, after Baron Marochetti's sculpture. This Parian was exhibited in London in 1862.*

PARIAN

In 1847 Cole founded 'Felix Summerly's Art Manufactures', a design and marketing operation which attracted skilled designers and modellers such as John Bell, whose designs for porcelain were made up to exacting specifications at Minton. Many of the products in the Summerly catalogue were executed in the new 'Parian', a porcelain-like body which was easy to clean and had the light-reflecting qualities of marble but not its chilling coldness. Parian replaced bisque, the body previously used for figures, which was prone to discolouration.

Using Cheverton's Reducing Machine (a type of pantograph), it became easier to make faithful reproductions of scaled-down Parian models of life-size classical sculptures. Contemporary models such as 'Dorothea', 'Clorinda', 'Miranda' and 'Una and the Lion' were produced for Summerly's. During the mid 1860s, when the popularity of white Parian began to wane, Minton introduced tinted Parian in chocolate, terracotta, salmon and green. The tinted clay was often used for drapery, but certain versions of 'Dorothea' were produced with white drapery and vivid green flesh! Over

five hundred different figure models were produced before Minton ceased to make Parian statuary about 1890, when it had become unfashionable. Parian figures were usually well marked. Those designed by John Bell incorporate his name and the 'FS' (Felix Summerly) monogram.

The 116-piece hand-pierced, hand-painted dessert service purchased by Queen Victoria at the Great Exhibition of 1851 combined bone-china dishes with allegorical figure supports in Parian (the cover

Below: *A reduced version in Parian of Colin Minton Campbell, figure number 501, after the bronze by Sir Thomas Brock which stands outside the Minton factory, 1887; 48.4 cm (19 inches).*

11

Tinted Parian figures of 'Science', number 470 (left), and 'Fine Art', number 469 (right), by Thomas Nelson Maclean. These figures were exhibited at Vienna in 1873. Height 37 cm (14¹/₂ inches).

photograph shows an example from the service). Each piece was painted with a different design, including cherubs by Thomas Kirkby, and figures, landscapes, fruit and flowers by Joseph Bancroft. Both Kirkby and Bancroft were Minton artists. The service took an entire year to complete. Queen Victoria presented the service to the Emperor of Austria and ordered a second set for her own use. Her Majesty introduced Herbert Minton to the Princess of Prussia as 'the manufacturer of that beautiful dessert service'. Minton was the only English manufacturer to be awarded the Council Bronze Medal for 'beauty and originality of design' at the Exhibition.

Left: *Earthenware block-printed dinner plate from the 'Proverbs' service designed by A. W. N. Pugin, inscribed 'It is a good tongue that says no ill, & a better heart that thinks none'; example dated c.1860.*

Right: *Encaustic bread tray inscribed 'Waste not want not', designed by A. W. N. Pugin and exhibited at the Birmingham Exhibition of 1849.*

PUGIN TABLEWARE

The Minton Archives contain many signed and dated tableware designs by Augustus Welby Northmore Pugin. Earthenware services with printed Pugin designs such as 'Medieval', 'Gothic' (a border and centre of trefoil crosses) and 'Proverbs', which had amusing borders, such as 'Eat thy bread with joy and drink thy wine with a merry heart', were the most popular. Pugin's personal Minton tableware produced for his marriage was inscribed *'ubi amor ibi fides'* ('Where there is love there is faith').

Earthenware block-printed dinner ware designed by A. W. N. Pugin, c.1850.

Encaustic floor tiles by A. W. N. Pugin, c.1850.

ENCAUSTIC TILES

Medieval floor tiles which had been unearthed at King's Lynn (Norfolk), St Mary Witton, near Droitwich (Worcestershire) and Great Malvern (Worcestershire) had fascinated Pugin, and Herbert Minton saw the revival of the tiles as a manufacturing challenge. Encouraged by Pugin, he pursued the idea, in spite of strong opposition from his partner, John Boyle, and was heard to retort: 'Say no more on the subject, Mr Boyle, I will make these tiles if they cost a guinea each!'

Block-printed decorative wall tiles, 1865. Block-printing, patented by Collins and Reynolds in 1848, provided printed decoration on ceramics in one or more colours

The technique required a red clay to be pressed into a plaster of Paris or brass mould with a raised design at the bottom. When this was removed, the design was left impressed into the clay surface. The impression was filled with liquid clay of a different colour and, when it was dry enough, it was scraped level, left to dry further and finally scraped and smoothed until level. To add strength and eliminate warping, a layer of coarse clay was inserted between two layers of best-quality clay.

One of the earliest Minton encaustic floors was supplied to Trentham Hall, Staffordshire, in 1830. Probably the finest examples, designed by Pugin, can be seen in the Houses of Parliament — in the Royal Gallery, the Central Lobby and St Stephen's Hall. These floors were completed between 1847 and 1852. Pugin wrote to Herbert Minton: 'I declare your St Stephen's tiles are the finest done in the tile way; vastly superior to any ancient work, in fact they are the best tiles in the world, and I think my patterns and your workmanship go ahead of anything.' Other Pugin examples can be seen at St George's Hall, Liverpool, and St Giles Roman Catholic Church, Cheadle, Staffordshire, known as 'Pugin's Gem'.

Encaustic tiles were up to an inch (25 mm) thick, with pierced holes on the reverse to facilitate drying and to key in the mortar. They were usually marked 'Minton & Co', or 'Minton's China Works, Stoke on Trent', and sometimes impressed year ciphers were added.

DUST-PRESSED AND BLOCK-PRINTED TILES

Two patents taken out in the 1840s were to revolutionise tile production. In 1840 Richard Prosser, a Birmingham engineer, patented the technique of dust-pressing, making articles from powdered clay under pressure, and in 1848 F.W.M. Collins and Alfred Reynolds patented the block-printing technique, which enabled flat areas of colour to be printed on the tile's surface. Multicoloured designs could also be produced by this method. Pugin made use of these new developments and early examples can be found in the Smoking Room at the House of Commons.

MAJOLICA

Léon Arnoux, the son of Antoine Arnoux who, with his brother-in-law Joseph Jacques Fouqué, established a pottery at Toulouse in 1800, came to Minton in about 1845. He introduced 'Majolica', brightly coloured lead-glazed wares. This type of ware originated in Spain and was carried to Italy in Majorcan vessels. It became known in Italy as *maiolica* and was reproduced by the Italians. Some Minton Majolica painted wares were exact copies of Italian tin-glazed *maiolica*. Minton Majolica can be divided into two categories: Italianate reproductions, and naturalistic Majolica

Above: *Revivalist plaque painted by Thomas Kirkby in 1860. This is a direct copy of the Roman soldier after Mantegna from the South Kensington Museum.*

Below: *Majolica glazed ewer modelled by Protât, c.1865.*

Above: *Majolica glazed 'Chinaman' teapot, c.1870.*

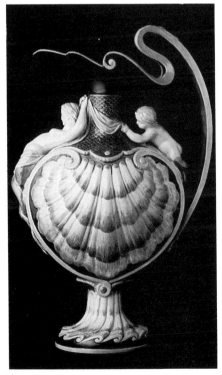

which uses nature as a design source. Minton *maiolica* reproductions include snake-handled vases painted with 'Justice', 'Theology', 'Philosophy' and 'Poetry' (after Raphael in the Stanza della Signatura in the Vatican). Other examples combined *maiolica*-style ornaments with contemporary portraits, such as the plaques designed by Silas Rice and painted by Thomas Kirkby, of Queen Victoria and the Empress Eugénie, which were framed with heavy scrollwork and grotesques.

The humour in naturalistic Majolica gave it a wide appeal. Models included: a 'Monkey Teapot', with removable head to form the lid; 'Cat and the Mouse Teapot', featuring a cat sitting on the handle watching the

Above left: 'Monkey Garden Seat', shape number 589, naturalistically modelled and decorated with Majolica glazes, c.1860; 47 cm (18½ inches).

Above right: Armchair garden seat produced in Majolica glazes, c.1865.

Left: Majolica male and female blackamoors, shape numbers 1157 and 1158, designed by Carrier de Belleuse in 1865; 180 cm (72 inches).

16

mouse emerge from a wedge of cheese; 'Game Pie Dish', one with rabbit and duck heads protruding from a basket base, and another modelled as a hollow tree trunk with foxes chasing ducks around the base; and a 'Cheese Dish', with a cheese infested with mice — some peeping out, and others disappearing into holes — surmounted by a mouse eating a lump of cheese.

Minton developed a special body for Majolica glazed furniture and large-scale ornaments such as armchairs, tables, 'Monkey Garden Seats', barrel-shaped seats, life-size fawns, storks, herons and the 5 foot (1.5 metre) tall peacock. One of the peacocks modelled by Paul Comolera was shipped to Australia, survived a shipwreck and emerged in perfect condition, after months under the sea; it is now exhibited in Flagstaff Hill Maritime Village, Warrnambool, Victoria. The most spectacular fountain was exhibited in 1862. Modelled by John Thomas and surmounted by St George and the dragon, it was 39 feet (11.9 metres) high and 40 feet (12.2 metres) in diameter.

Majolica and other ornamental wares have one or many of the following marks: impressed year cipher; impressed MINTON (before 1873) or MINTONS (after 1873); and an impressed number of three or four digits, which correspond to the numbers in the Minton ornamental shape books.

MAJOLICA TILES

From the 1860s relief-moulded Majolica glazed tiles added a new dimension to interiors. Large-scale decorative schemes incorporating Majolica tiles were executed at the Foreign Office in London, the Royal Dairy at Frogmore, near Windsor, Berkshire, and the Gamble Room and the ceramic staircase at the South Kensington Museum (now the Victoria and Albert Museum) in London. Majolica glazed tiles remained in production until Art Nouveau slip-trailed tiles became popular around 1900. From about 1870 the globe with a ribbon emblazoned with 'Stoke upon Trent' and 'Walbrook London' was often used. 'England' was added in 1891.

In 1856 Herbert Minton was appointed a Royal Warrant holder and gained the personal distinction of Chevalier of the Order of the Legion of Honour of France. He died in 1858, having seen the factory grow in his lifetime, both in the numbers of his workforce (which totalled 1500) and in international stature.

This life-size Majolica glazed earthenware peacock, modelled by Paul Comolera in 1873, is displayed in the Minton Museum. 152.4 cm (61 inches).

Above left: 'Vase Rothschild' triangular shape with pierced cover in bleu-celeste ground, after Sèvres vase triangulaire, c.1855; 38 cm (15 inches).

Above right: Pair of perforated chain-handle vases, shape number 469, after Sèvres models, c.1870, 38 cm (15 inches).

Below: Bone-china ewers and vase, turquoise ground, decorated in enamel colours, outlined in gold, designed by Christopher Dresser, c.1870.

*(Left) Bone-china pseudo-cloisonné vases and jardinière designed by Christopher Dresser, 1870.
(Extreme right) Bone-china lidded jar, weighted to simulate metal — a direct copy of Japanese
cloisonné, 1870.*

COLIN MINTON CAMPBELL — PIONEER OF
THE ART POTTERY STUDIO

Herbert Minton had no children and after his death the factory was taken over by his nephew, Colin Minton Campbell. Colin Minton Campbell was also an innovator and he continued to attract influential designers such as Christopher Dresser and to introduce new techniques such as the acid gold process and *pâte-sur-pâte*. Colin Minton Campbell was a pioneer of the art pottery movement and he opened a London studio for Minton in 1871.

From the 1860s Christopher Dresser had a notable influence on Minton shapes and surface decoration. He developed many unique ornamental shapes for Minton based on spheres, cylinders and cones, which were used to create strikingly original pieces. Dresser trained as a botanist and this detailed knowledge, together with his love of the grotesque, is evident in designs incorporating the scarab beetle, grasshoppers, spiders and frogs. To temper the grotesque element, Dresser often introduced humour, for example, when he made a face out of the markings on a beetle's back! His best known design was of Japanese cranes flying past the sun and over the waves, inspired by Hokusai's 'Great Wave' painting.

Other strong influences were eighteenth-century Sèvres wares and Japanese art. The latter influence was further stimulated by the display of Japanese cloisonné wares exhibited at the London Exhibition of 1862. Minton produced 'pseudo-cloisonné' wares soon afterwards, having already perfected the required ground colours of turquoise, pink and yellow. Minton's pseudo-cloisonné was decorated with Japanese-style motifs outlined in gold, and some examples were weighted to simulate metal.

Right: *Earthenware U-shape flower holder, designed by Christopher Dresser, c.1870.*

Far right: *'Vase Hollandaise', rose Pompadour ground, shape number 2185, after a Sèvres model, 1900, 21 cm (8¹/4 inches).*

ACID GOLD PROCESS

In 1863 James Leigh Hughes, a Minton gilder, was granted letters patent for the acid gold process, an invention which added a new dimension to tableware, providing a bas-relief gold finish. In the process hydrofluoric acid was used to etch a pattern in the glaze which was then filled with 22 carat gold. The technique was most suited to decorative borders and crests but could be applied all over the china to give a rich exotic effect. Colin Minton Campbell was quick to acquire the patent rights and the technique has since been used in over a thousand patterns. The earliest example was the dessert service commissioned in 1865 by Lord Milton, the son of Earl Fitzwilliam. This incorporated his coronet and monogram in acid gold. The service commemorated Lord Milton's safe return from an expedition from the Atlantic to the Pacific, undertaken to explore a route across Canada to British Columbia, through British territory, by one of the northern passes in the Rocky mountains.

Below: *Two examples from Lord Milton's dessert service commemorating his safe return from a hazardous expedition to discover a north-west passage across Canada, 1865.*

PÂTE-SUR-PÂTE

Minton's greatest contribution to Victorian ceramics was the *pâte-sur-pâte* (paste on paste) decorative technique perfected by Louis Marc Emmanuel Solon, who came to Minton from France in 1870. Solon applied slip (liquid clay) in successive layers, gradually building up an image on to a tinted Parian body, in its clay state. These painted layers of white or polychrome slip were applied to the pot when it was 'workable' (preserved in a damp state whilst in the process of decoration). When the limbs of a figure had been gradually built up, translucent drapery and floating veils were often added, this translucency being the hallmark of a successful work in *pâte-sur-pâte*. These gossamer applications of slip can be seen in a maiden's silk veil, the wing of a dragonfly, smoke, clouds or clear water. Solon's white *pâte-sur-pâte* on bronze ground was described by him as 'resembling clouds of thick cream in a cup of dark tea'.

Solon designed complex shapes in strong ground colours of peacock blue, olive, bronze-green, dark brown, red-brown and 'changing pink' (or artificial ruby) which gave more depth and tone, particularly to the applied layers of white slip. Artificial ruby was obtained by a combination of bichromate of potash and alumina to give a pink which intensified when subjected to artificial light. Blue or green added to this caused the pink colour to be hidden during the daylight but at night the blue or green disappeared and the body became a deep carmine.

Solon drew his inspiration from Greek vases and terracottas which he had studied at the Cluny Museum, Paris, but his compositions were original and spontaneous and were enhanced by his great sense of humour.

Subjects were based on the many facets of love, for example 'Love Bored', 'Barometer of Love', 'Love's Toll Barrier' and 'Hope Feeding Love'. Other favourite subjects featured the elements, and cherubs performing sporting activities: 'Fishing', 'Athlete and Juggler', 'The Acrobat', 'Tug of War' and 'Darts'. The execution of Solon's work varied greatly: 'The Planning of the Journey' took 25 days, whilst

Left: Pair of pâte-sur-pâte vases, shape number 1653, decorated by Louis Solon, with Cupid imprisoned and Cupid escaping, c.1890.

Right: Slab, depicting 'Roman Nouveau', in pâte-sur-pâte, by Louis Solon, c.1890.

Pâte-sur-pâte decorated ornamental wares by Louis Solon, with tinted Parian ground colours of olive green, salmon, chocolate and peacock blue, dated between 1880 and 1890.

Hand-pierced dessert plate and tea cup and saucer decorated with pâte-sur-pâte cherubs by Alboin Birks, c.1890.

Above: *Tug-of-war pâte-sur-pâte panel by Louis Solon.*

Right: *Font, decorated in pâte-sur-pâte by Louis Solon, the leading exponent of the technique, with cherub support modelled by Carrier de Belleuse; 60.96 cm (24 inches).*

'Lycurgus and the Wrestling Girls of Sparta' took seven months.

Solon was assisted by a small number of apprentices, namely Alboin Birks, Lawrence Birks, Frederick Rhead, Henry Sanders, William Morgan, Thomas Rice, Thomas Mellor and Richard Bradbury. Examples of *pâte-sur-pâte* were signed by incising the slip with the end of a brush and were well marked on the reverse with a gold-printed globe backstamp and the usual year ciphers and shape numbers.

MINTON'S LONDON ART POTTERY STUDIO

Minton had been supplying 'blanks' (undecorated ware) to the South Kensington Museum (now the Victoria and Albert Museum) painting classes since the 1860s. These were painted by the students to designs by Edward J. Poynter and installed at the Grill Room of the museum. The success of this exercise prompted Colin Minton Campbell to lease a plot of ground on the Gore estate in order to build a studio to decorate and fire earthenware blanks produced at Stoke. Minton's Art Pottery Studio was opened in 1871. Situated between the Royal Albert Hall and the Horticultural Gardens, it was close to the South Kensington Museum and the School of Art, which enabled the artists to study both from historical sources and from nature.

Below: *Art Pottery Studio plaque freely painted by William Stephen Coleman, 1871.*

23

Above: *Earthenware plaque depicting a girl with a lizard, painted by William Stephen Coleman at Minton's Art Pottery Studio, Kensington Gore, 1871, 42.5 cm (16³/4 inches).*

Above: *Plaque painted by Herbert Wilson Foster in the Art Pottery Studio style, 1879; 30.2 cm (12 inches).*

Right: *Art Pottery Studio flask painted with a female head by Eliza Jameson Strutt, 1872. Other students painted the decorative borders.*

William Stephen Coleman, a naturalist, talented artist, author and book illustrator, who joined Minton in 1869, was chosen to be director of the Studio. The earliest Studio productions were influenced by Coleman's freely artistic and distinctive style. His colourful naturalistic designs featured birds, flowers, butterflies, cherubs, children, and maidens who were often very scantily clad. Favourite compositions (usually featuring the Minton turquoise, which he admired) included cherubs with nets chasing butterflies, tropical plants, fish, young girls perched on the branches of trees and sensual portrayals of reclining maidens on leopard skins, holding bubbles, tambourines and lizards.

Studio wares included moon flasks, pilgrim bottles, jardinières, spill vases, tiles, panels and plaques. These were decorated by the students under the supervision of Coleman and others, including Edmond Reuter, William Wise, William Mussill and George Woolliscroft Rhead. The freelance designers Henry Stacy Marks and John Moyr Smith supplied innovative designs based on revived medievalism, whilst Christopher Dresser's contributions were in humorous vein.

Many important commissions were successfully completed in the first year, but Coleman lost the commission to decorate the Criterion Theatre by failing to complete the work in time. In 1873 he withdrew from the arduous task of managing the Studio, preferring to submerge himself in his painting. John Eyre took over as manager and soon afterwards Matthew Elden replaced Coleman as director. Elden's designs were unpopular and he resorted to making inferior copies of Coleman's works, much to the disapproval of Colin Minton Campbell, who attempted to preserve the prestige of the Studio by persuading the artists to reproduce photographic work of theatrical characters. These 'photographic' plaques, particularly the work of Herbert Wilson Foster, who painted 'Sarah Bernhardt', 'Henry Irving', 'Madame Désirée with Fan', 'Wife of Rembrandt' and 'Ophelia', became extremely popular.

In 1875 a disastrous fire completely destroyed the Studio and Campbell decided that it was not financially viable to rebuild. However, Coleman's designs and decorative tiles and panels continued to be produced in Stoke into the 1890s.

Studio wares were marked on the reverse with a special printed backstamp, 'Minton's Art Pottery Studio, Kensington Gore', and with painted monograms of the students, impressed shape numbers and impressed year ciphers.

PRINTED TILE SERIES

The influence of the aesthetic movement of the 1870s brought a dramatic increase in the use of decorative panels and wall tiles. Block-printed picture tiles designed by John Moyr Smith depicting Shakespeare's plays and Tennyson's *Idylls of the King* were popular.

In his lifetime Colin Minton Campbell had seen Minton well established throughout the world, their position enhanced by successes at international exhibitions. After his death in 1885 the factory remained under family control, but the company suffered the loss of his great leadership. Production centred on past styles, in particular a revival of the Sèvres-inspired ornamental wares and tablewares. The quality of the potting and the painting of Antonin Boullemier, James Edwin Dean, Albert Gregory and Richard Pilsbury was superlative. In 1895 Minton responded to the Art Nouveau style by securing the services of Léon Solon, son of Louis Solon of *pâte-sur-pâte* fame, grandson of Léon Arnoux and continued their prestigious course into the twentieth century.

A selection of decorative wall tiles. (Top left) Multi-coloured block-printed tile in the Japanese style, c.1870. (Top right) Blue and white painted wildlife subjects, number S1151, Minton's Art Pottery Studio, c.1872. (Bottom left) 'The Lion and the Rat' from Aesop's Fables, c.1875. (Bottom right) Probably from the 'Village Life' series designed by William Wise, c.1885.

25

Left to right: *Two Art Nouveau vases, inverted trumpet shape, designed by Léon Solon, 1902, the first with slip-trailed decoration, the second with block-printed decoration. Earthenware 'Secessionist ware' vase with slip-trailed decoration designed by Léon Solon and John Wadsworth, 1902. Height of all three vases, 30 cm (12 inches).*

THE TWENTIETH CENTURY

Minton were quick to adopt the Art Nouveau style, which made its first appearance at La Maison de l'Art Nouveau in Paris in the mid 1890s, although sinuous and curvaceous decoration was evident before this date. Art Nouveau was based upon the European arts and crafts and aesthetic movements and was promoted by periodicals such as *The Studio*, *L'Art Décoratif*, *Pan* and *Kunst und Kunsthandwerk*, and through exhibitions of art and design. Léon Solon's designs were featured in *The Studio* while he was still a student, and the magazine continued to follow his work for Minton with interest. He interpreted the florid linear style most effectively on tiles and earthenware ornamental wares. His sinuous, foliate and figurative designs accentuated with relief-moulded edges were applied to new elongated shapes.

SECESSIONIST WARE

In 1902, with his co-designer John Wadsworth, he introduced 'Secessionist ware', so called because of its fashionable connotations with the Viennese Secession Movement. Its elongated ornamental shapes were either relief-moulded or slip-trailed (piped with liquid clay to form a raised outline) and coloured with red, green, ochre, purple and turquoise glazes, which were painted within the outlines. Secessionist ware was produced in considerable quantities; many vases have survived, but candlesticks, toiletwares, dessert sets, tea and coffee pots and cheese dishes are more rarely found. Secessionist ware was marked with special printed 'Mintons Ltd' backstamps and printed numbers which relate to the designs.

Left: *Earthenware 'Secessionist ware' jardinière with block-printed and relief-moulded decoration, coloured with lead glazes, designed by Léon Solon, 1902.*

Right: *Earthenware 'Byzantine' flower vase, with stippled blue ground painted in enamels and gilt, c.1930.*

ART DECO

Minton was slow to adopt the clean-cut, bold, geometric Art Deco style. In the 1930s Reginald George Haggar created geometric and faceted vases entitled 'Les Vases Modernes' and the light-hearted tableware designs of 'Mexican', based on modern art, 'Toy Soldiers' and 'Noah's Ark', painted in a primitive style.

Minton produced the revolutionary cube-shape tea and coffee ware for use in cafés and restaurants, specifically to make storage easier and reduce breakages, because of the lack of projecting parts. These were

1930s figures. (Left) 'Little Mother' by Richard Bradbury. (Centre) 'The Bather' by Doris Lindner. (Right) 'Waiter' napkin-holder figure.

Bone-china 'cube' shape stacking set, painted in enamels with 'Cuckoo' pattern for the Cunard steamship line, c.1930.

supplied to the Cunard steamship line and Lyons coffee houses. Stylish Art Deco figures, including 'The Bather' by Doris Lindner, 'The Hikers' by Eric Owen and cartoon-like figures with enormously bowed legs used as napkin holders, were produced in the 1930s.

In 1935 John Wadsworth introduced pastel-coloured 'Solano' glazed earthenware tableware, with stencilled designs of leaves, spots, stripes, diamonds or swirls in white. Examples were named on the reverse, together with a facsimile of his signature. Kitchen ware with brightly coloured bands and lettering, vases decorated with 'drip' glazes and stylish lamps fitted for electricity were also produced. Wadsworth also designed 'Byzantine', 'Rotique' and 'Tulippa' ware, decorated in a choice of stippled ground colours with printed and enamelled borders, and commemoratives marking significant events during the reigns of Edward VIII and George VI and the coronation of Elizabeth II.

During the Second World War restrictions were placed on the pottery industry by the government: only plain undecorated wares could be supplied to the home mar-

Earthenware 'Tulippa' plaque and 'Rotique' tazza, produced in blue, green, pink and brown stippled grounds, and painted in enamel colours and gilding, c.1930.

28

ket, whilst decorated china was permitted only for certain export markets. Restrictions were not relaxed until 1952.

'Haddon Hall', a pretty all-over pink, green and yellow chinoiserie pattern with a green edge on the fluted shape, was introduced by Wadsworth in 1949 and remains today Minton's best-selling pattern.

In celebration of the coronation of Elizabeth II in 1953, the British Pottery Manufacturers' Federation presented a vase to the Queen. John Wadsworth designed the 2 foot (60 cm) tall vase, which was decorated with symbols of all the Commonwealth nations and the four countries of the British Isles around its ten sides. The ten alcoves in the sides housed the Queen's Beasts. Minton produced limited editions of the Queen's Beasts two years later.

John Wadsworth died in 1955 and in 1957 Douglas Henson was appointed chief designer. He created the contemporary 'Monarch' shape and the best-selling 'Bellemeade' pattern, amongst others.

By 1968 Minton was under considerable pressure to re-equip with new plant and machinery. The cost of this was high and the profit from tableware was small, and the decision was taken to merge with Royal Doulton, whose productions were complementary, and whose resources in design and commerce would maintain Minton's worldwide reputation. Many new Minton patterns were designed by Joseph Ledger, then director of design at Royal Doulton, and his art directors, at the time Monica Ford and Walter Hayward. Joseph Ledger designed the 'Granville' shape and 'St James' pattern, Monica Ford produced 'Grasmere', and Walter Hayward created 'Consort'. Patterns introduced in the 1990s have included Barry Meeson's 'Birds of Paradise', Bobbie Clayton's 'Tapestry' and Marilyn Hankinson's 'Caliph'.

This best-selling pattern, 'Haddon Hall', was designed by John Wadsworth in 1949.

Bone-china vase, with emerald, black and gold stylised lotus, one of a collection designed by John Wadsworth, c.1940.

Minton's figurative traditions continued in 1979 when cast bronze and ivory china figures were designed by Eric Griffiths. The eleven subjects included 'Sea Breezes', 'The Fisherman' and 'The Sheik'. The figures were discontinued in 1984. In 1991 Robert Jefferson produced limited editions

29

of bisque and glazed white and gilt contemporary figures, based on classical sources, entitled 'Amphitrite and the Dolphin', 'Galatea and the River', 'Hera and the Peacock', and 'Leda and the Swan'.

Throughout Minton's history freelance designers have been associated with the company and in 1987 Jean Muir, the celebrated designer of clothes, created a collection of octagonal boxes, trays and vases for use in the office or boudoir, based on textile designs.

Using the artwork and pattern books from the unique archives as a foundation on which to build designs for today, Kenneth Wright, the design manager, created the 'Contrasts' coffee-can collection, which was based on Pugin's designs, and 'Donovan Bird', which is a supreme example of an interpretation of number 51 from the first pattern book.

Minton's raised-paste gold work and hand-painted commissions are acknowledged to be first-class. As they have been for two hundred years, traditional skills are still combined with the innovative designs for which the name of Minton remains in high esteem.

Bronze and ceramic 'Sea Breezes', one of a series of eleven figures designed by Eric Griffiths between 1979 and 1981.

FURTHER READING

Atterbury, P., and Batkin, M. *The Dictionary of Minton*. Antique Collectors' Club, 1990.

Atterbury, P. (editor). *The Parian Phenomenon*. Dennis, 1989.

Atterbury, P., and Wainwright, C. *Pugin, A Gothic Passion*. Yale University Press, 1994.

Barker, D. *Parian Ware*. Shire, 1985.

Beaulah, K. *Church Tiles of the Nineteenth Century*. Shire, 1987.

Bergesen, V. *Majolica British, Continental and American Wares, 1851-1915*. Barrie and Jenkins, 1989.

Dawes, N. M. *Majolica*. Crown, New York, 1990.

Godden, G. A. *Minton Pottery and Porcelain of the First Period 1793-1850*. Herbert Jenkins, 1968.

Halén, W. *Christopher Dresser*. Phaidon, 1990.

Henrywood, R. K. *Relief Moulded Jugs*. Antique Collectors' Club, 1985.

Holt, G. *A Cup of Tea*. Pavilion, 1991. First period Minton tea cups and saucers illustrated.

Jones, J. *Minton: The First Two Hundred Years of Design and Production*. Swan Hill Press, 1993.

Karmason, M. G., and Stacke, J. B. *Majolica: A Complete History and Illustrated Survey*. Abrams, New York, 1989.

Lockett, T. A. *Collecting Victorian Tiles*. Antique Collectors' Club, 1979.

Skinner, D. S., and Van Lemmen, H. *Minton Tiles 1835-1985*. Stoke-on-Trent City Museum, 1984.

Spours, J. *Art Deco Tableware*. Ward Lock, 1988.

Van Lemmen, H. *Victorian Tiles*. Shire, 1981, updated 1989.

SOME MINTON MARKS

Painted Sèvres-type, c.1800-16; bone china

Printed, c. 1824-36; earthenware

Printed, c. 1824-36; felspar porcelain

Printed, c. 1824-36; felspar porcelain

Moulded, c.1830-60; stoneware, Parian and earthenware

Printed, 1826-41(Minton & Boyle); earthenware

B.B.

Impressed (meaning 'best body'), c. 1830-50; earthenware

Printed, c.1841-50; earthenware

Printed, 1845-68 (Minton & Hollins); earthenware

Ermine (incised, painted or printed), c. 1845-65; bone china and parian

Moulded Summerly mark, c. 1846-56; parian designed by John Bell for Summerly's Art Manufactures

Printed, c. 1850-70; high-quality earthenware and porcelain

Printed, c. 1870; bone china and earthenware decorated with Coleman's 'Naturalist' motifs

MINTONS
Art-Pottery
STUDIO
Kensington
Gore

MINTONS
Art-Pottery
STUDIO
Kensington
Gore

Printed, c. 1871-75; wares decorated at Mintons Art Pottery Studio

Printed; wares for 1878 Paris Exhibition

18
(MINTON)
72

Impressed, c.1868-80, includes date manufactured (1872); Sèvres-type porcelains

Printed, c. 1902-14; Secessionist ware

Minton
MINTON
MINTONS

Impressed (usually with impressed year cyphers), c. 1860-1910, Mintons after 1873; all types

Printed globe from 1863 - Mintons with a crown after 1873, 'England' from 1891, 'Made in England' from c.1920; all types

MINTONS
ENGLAND

Impressed or moulded, c.1890-1910

Printed, from 1951, including pattern number and name; bone china

MINTON
CHINA
3.66.

Impressed, showing last two figures of date of manufacture - here 1966; bone china

Printed; present day

PLACES TO VISIT

Museum displays may be altered and readers are advised to telephone before visiting to check that relevant items are on show, as well as to find out the opening times.

GREAT BRITAIN

Birmingham Museum and Art Gallery, Chamberlain Square, Birmingham, West Midlands B3 3DH. Telephone: 0121-235 2834. Varied Minton collection — check collection availability before visit.

The British Museum, Great Russell Street, London WC1B 3DG. Telephone: 0171-636 1555.

Gladstone Pottery Museum, 26 Uttoxeter Road, Longton, Stoke-on-Trent, Staffordshire ST3 1PQ. Telephone: 01782 311378 or 319232.

Lichfield Cathedral, Lichfield, Staffordshire. Telephone: 01543 256120. Minton floor tiles.

Liverpool Museum, William Brown Street, Liverpool, Merseyside L3 8EN. Telephone: 0151-207 0001. Majolica peacock on display.

Manchester City Art Gallery, Mosley Street, Manchester M2 3JL. Telephone: 0161-236 5244. Varied Minton collection — check collection availability before visiting.

Minton Museum, Royal Doulton Limited, Minton House, London Road, Stoke-on-Trent, Staffordshire ST4 7QD. Telephone: 01782 292292. Comprehensive Minton collection from 1800 to the present day. Minton Archives available by appointment to serious researchers.

Paisley Museum and Art Galleries, High Street, Paisley, Renfrewshire PA1 2BA. Telephone: 0141-889 3151. Collection includes *pâte-sur-pâte*.

Royal Museum of Scotland, Chambers Street, Edinburgh EH1 1JF. Telephone: 0131-225 7534. Varied Minton Collection — check collection availability before visit.

St Giles Roman Catholic Church, Cheadle, Stoke-on-Trent, Staffordshire. Telephone: 01538 753130. By appointment. Pugin church, Minton tiles.

Stoke-on-Trent City Museum and Art Gallery, Bethesda Street, Hanley, Stoke-on-Trent, Staffordshire ST1 3DE. Telephone: 01782 202173. Varied Minton collection including Majolica garden furniture.

Thomas Goode and Company Limited, 19 South Audley Street, Grosvenor Square, London W1Y 6BN. Telephone: 0171-499 2823. Minton *tour-de-force* elephants.

Victoria and Albert Museum, Cromwell Road, South Kensington, London SW7 2RL. Telephone: 0171-938 8500. Minton Majolica tiles in the Silver Galleries and Staircase, Old Grill Room and Refreshment Room.

AUSTRALIA

Flagstaff Hill Maritime Village, Merri Street, Warrnambool 3280, Victoria. Minton peacock on display.

Power House Museum, Sydney, New South Wales. Varied collection of Minton including peacock.

CANADA

George R. Gardiner Museum of Ceramic Art, 111 Queen's Park, Toronto, Ontario M5S 2C7. Cumming Collection of first period Minton.

UNITED STATES OF AMERICA

Cooper-Hewitt Museum, The Smithsonian Institution's National Museum of Design, 2 East 91st Street, New York, NY 10028.

Metropolitan Museum of Art, 5th Avenue at 82nd Street, New York, NY 10028.

Philadelphia Museum of Art, 26th Street and Benjamin Franklin Parkway, Philadelphia, Pennsylvania 19101.